Assessing the Short-Term Effects on Output of Changes in Federal Fiscal Policies

Changes in federal fiscal policies can have both short-term and long-term effects on output. The Congressional Budget Office's analysis of the short-term effects focuses on the impact on the demand for goods and services. That impact can be decomposed into direct effects and indirect effects: Direct effects consist of changes in purchases of goods and services by federal agencies and by the people and organizations who are recipients of federal payments or payers of federal taxes; indirect effects enhance or offset the direct effects. The indirect effects can be summarized by a demand multiplier, defined as the total change in gross domestic product per dollar of direct effect on demand. This paper presents the ranges of demand multipliers that CBO uses in its analyses and reviews evidence on the size of those multipliers.

I. Introduction

Changes in federal fiscal policies—which can take the form of changes in federal spending, taxes, or both—can have both short-term and long-term effects on the economy. In the short term, the economy's output can deviate from its potential level (a level that corresponds to a high rate of use of labor and capital) in response to changes in demand for goods and services by consumers, businesses, governments, and foreigners. Tax cuts and increases in government spending can boost demand, which encourages businesses to gear up production and hire more workers than they otherwise would; tax increases and spending cuts can reduce demand, which has the opposite effects.

In the long term, the key determinant of output is the economy's potential to produce goods and services—which depends on the size and quality of the labor force, on the stock of productive capital, and on the efficiency with which labor and capital are used to produce goods and services. Changes in taxes and spending affect potential output primarily by affecting the amount of public saving and the incentives for individuals and businesses to work, save, and invest.

The Congressional Budget Office (CBO) analyzes the economic effects of proposed changes in federal fiscal policies in both the short term and the long term.[1] The agency's analysis of the short-term effects focuses on the impact on the demand for goods and services. That impact can be decomposed into direct effects and indirect effects.

Direct effects consist of changes in purchases of goods and services by federal agencies and by the people and organizations who are recipients of federal payments or payers of federal taxes. The size of the direct effects of a change in policies depends on the behavior of those recipients and payers. For example, if someone receives a dollar in transfer payments and spends 80 cents (saving the other 20 cents), production increases over time to meet the additional demand generated by that spending, and the direct impact on output is 80 cents; if someone receives a dollar and spends less than 80 cents, the direct impact on production would be proportionately smaller. Accordingly, CBO has reviewed evidence on the responses of households, businesses, and government to various types of tax cuts and transfer payments to estimate the size of those policies' direct effects on output.[2]

Indirect effects of changes in fiscal policies enhance or offset the direct effects. For example, direct effects are enhanced when an initial increase in spending raises employment and those who are hired use their income to boost consumption. Direct effects also are enhanced when an increase in

---

[1] For examples and more-detailed discussions of CBO's approach to such analyses, see Congressional Budget Office (2010a; 2011a; 2011b; 2012b; 2012c; 2012d).

[2] For instance, CBO has developed estimates of the direct effect for each of the major classes of provisions in the American Recovery and Reinvestment Act (ARRA). See Congressional Budget Office (2012b).

spending prompts companies to increase investment to boost their future production. As an example in the other direction, direct effects are offset when an initial increase in spending leads to higher interest rates that discourage spending on investment and on durable goods such as cars because they raise the cost of borrowing by households and businesses.

The indirect effects can be summarized by a demand multiplier, defined as the total change in gross domestic product (GDP) for each dollar of direct effect on demand. CBO's analysis applies the same demand multiplier to any $1 of direct effect from a change in fiscal policies, regardless of the specific change in policies (for example, a tax cut or an increase in government spending). In the case of a multiplier greater than 1, the indirect effects enhance the direct effects; in the case of a multiplier less than 1, the indirect effects offset (or, in the case of a tax cut or increase in spending, "crowd out") some of the direct effects. A demand multiplier of zero would indicate that a direct effect is fully offset by the indirect effects; in that case, changes in fiscal policies would have no effect on GDP.

The product of a direct effect and a demand multiplier is sometimes referred to as an output multiplier or fiscal multiplier. Output multipliers differ across different fiscal policies because the direct effects differ. A change in federal purchases has a direct effect of 1, so the output multiplier for federal purchases equals the demand multiplier; most other changes in fiscal policies have direct effects that are less than 1 (because recipients of benefits and payers of taxes tend to adjust their spending less than one-for-one with changes in their income), in which case their output multipliers are smaller than the demand multiplier.

CBO's analyses generally use a range of values for the demand multiplier to reflect the uncertainty about its size. In addition, the range of estimates used by CBO varies with the degree of resource utilization in the economy and the response of monetary policy during the periods when the changes in fiscal policies occur. When actual output is well below potential output and the Federal Reserve does not act to offset the effects of changes in fiscal policies, CBO's demand multiplier ranges from 0.5 to 2.5 over four quarters, starting the quarter in which a direct effect occurs in response to changes in policies, with no further effects on output in the short term.[3]

When actual output is close to potential output and the Federal Reserve attempts to counteract the effects of changes in fiscal policies, CBO's demand multiplier ranges from 0.4 to 1.9 over those same four quarters. Under those circumstances, however, the economic impact of changes in interest rates grows over time, and output in the following four quarters moves in the opposite direction of its initial change. For policies with positive direct effects, GDP in the fifth quarter through the eighth quarter would be lower than the amount that would have been produced in the absence of the policies; and for policies with negative direct effects, GDP in those quarters would be higher than the amount that would have been produced in the absence of the policies. As a result, under those circumstances, CBO's demand multiplier falls to 0.2 to 0.8 over eight quarters.

II. Key Issues in Assessing Demand Multipliers

The size of the demand multiplier depends on the underlying features of the economy and on contemporaneous economic conditions, including the degree to which the economy's resources are utilized and the policy responses of the Federal Reserve (such as changes in the federal funds rate, an interest rate on overnight lending among banks that the Federal Reserve adjusts to conduct

---

[3] Over time, the amount of output is affected by the impact of the changes in fiscal policies on labor supply, the capital stock, and the efficiency with which labor and capital are combined. Changes in fiscal policies that aim to increase demand, such as increases in government purchases or reductions in taxes, are likely to decrease output in the long term relative to what it would be in the absence of those policies. That occurs because increases in government borrowing tend to eventually reduce the nation's saving and capital stock. Therefore, policies that increase demand often involve a trade-off between boosting economic output in the short term and reducing output in the long term. For further discussion of such trade-offs, see Congressional Budget Office (2012c).

monetary policy).[4] For example, when the economy is weak and resources are significantly underutilized, fiscal stimulus—which can take the form of increases in government spending or decreases in taxes—would likely be magnified by higher spending by the private sector, in which case the demand multiplier would be greater than 1. In that economic environment, because labor and capital would not be particularly scarce, a fiscal stimulus would be less likely to bid up the price of the economy's resources, and the Federal Reserve would be less likely to increase the federal funds rate. Indeed, the Federal Reserve has kept short-term interest rates near zero as federal fiscal policymakers have adopted stimulus measures during and after the recession that ended in June 2009.[5] As a result, CBO's estimates of the short-term economic effects of the American Recovery and Reinvestment Act of 2009 (ARRA), as well as the agency's estimates of the short-term economic effects of other changes in fiscal policies that have been considered recently, include little offset from increases in short-term interest rates.[6]

In contrast, when the economy's labor and capital resources are closer to being fully utilized, the direct effect of a fiscal stimulus would likely be offset in part by a reduction in spending that would have occurred in the absence of the stimulus. Because stimulus under those conditions increases inflationary pressures, the Federal Reserve would typically increase the federal funds rate, which combats inflation by raising the cost of borrowing and return to saving and thereby discouraging some spending. In those circumstances, the demand multiplier would likely be less than 1. Because

---

[4] See, for example, Parker (2011). The size of the demand multiplier may depend on other factors as well. For example, a very high amount of economic uncertainty can temporarily restrain economic activity and would likely reduce the multiplier in the short term; see Bloom (2009). The duration and timing of fiscal policy actions may also affect the size of the multiplier; see, for example, Coenen and coauthors (2012) and Christiano and coauthors (2011).

[5] From the fourth quarter of 2007 through the second quarter of 2009 (that is, from the peak of the previous expansion to the end of the recession), the Federal Reserve decreased the federal funds rate from 4.5 percent to 0.2 percent. Between the second quarter of 2009 and the first quarter of 2012, the federal funds rate averaged 0.1 percent, and the Federal Reserve announced in January 2012 (and reiterated its views as recently as April of this year) that it expects economic conditions will warrant exceptionally low levels for the federal funds rate at least through late 2014; see www.federalreserve.gov/newsevents/press/monetary/20120125a.htm. For further discussion of the weak economy, see Congressional Budget Office (2012a), pp. 25–26.

[6] See Congressional Budget Office (2011a; 2012b).

CBO expects that the economic effects of changes in fiscal policies are roughly symmetric—meaning that under similar economic conditions the size of the demand multiplier is the same for stimulative policies (such as increases in government spending or decreases in taxes) as for contractionary policies (such as decreases in government spending or increases in taxes)—the economic effects of contractionary policies would similarly be larger during times of low resource utilization than during times of full resource utilization.[7]

Observing economic outcomes following changes in fiscal policies does not allow researchers to determine the size of the demand multiplier with certainty because that would require knowing what path the economy would have taken in the absence of a given policy action. Therefore, analyzing data on output and employment after a change in fiscal policy takes effect is not as helpful in determining the policy's economic consequences as might be supposed. To reflect the uncertainty involved in estimates of the demand multiplier—and the resulting disagreement among economists about the size of the multiplier—CBO generally uses ranges of demand multipliers in its analyses. CBO chooses those ranges judgmentally to try to encompass most economists' views.

CBO bases its ranges for the demand multiplier on three sources of information, each with its own strengths and limitations. CBO relies most heavily on results from macroeconometric forecasting models, but it also uses results from time series models and dynamic general-equilibrium models. Those models differ in their emphasis on economic theory and their reliance on historical data. Macroeconometric forecasting models incorporate relationships among aggregate economic variables that are based on both historical data and economic theory. Time series models rely heavily on historical data and place less emphasis on economic theory; they document the

---

[7] See Congressional Budget Office (2011b). For different perspectives on the economic effects of fiscal contractions, see International Monetary Fund (2010) and Alesina and Ardagna (1998).

historical correlation between fiscal policy and measures of aggregate economic activity. Dynamic general-equilibrium models rely less on historical data and place greater emphasis on economic theory; such models are labeled dynamic because they focus on how an economy evolves over time.

The demand multipliers used by CBO represent the total change in GDP for each dollar of direct effect on demand. The multipliers reported in this paper generally refer to the effect on GDP over four quarters, starting the quarter in which a direct effect occurs in response to changes in policies; in some places, this paper also addresses multipliers over eight quarters. When interpreting the results of academic research on demand multipliers, it is important to note that the definition of "multiplier" differs from study to study. For example, reported multipliers are sometimes "peak" multipliers (which represent the largest effect on output in any one quarter after a policy) or "instantaneous" multipliers (which represent the effect on output in a given quarter after a policy). Unless otherwise noted, and consistent with the focus of much of the economics literature, multipliers cited in this paper are estimated assuming what might be termed "normal" economic conditions—that is, when Federal Reserve policy operates without the restraint of a zero lower bound on the federal funds rate.

III. The Demand Multipliers Used by CBO

CBO uses demand multipliers that range from 0.4 to 1.9 over four quarters when the Federal Reserve responds to the inflationary pressures that arise from an increase in aggregate demand in one quarter (such as that from fiscal stimulus) by raising short-term interest rates. As the economic impact of changes in interest rates grows over time, output in the following four quarters falls below the amount that would have been produced in the absence of the initial increase in aggregate demand. Therefore, when the total effects on GDP are cumulated over eight quarters instead of four, the demand multipliers range from 0.2 to 0.8. Those ranges are broadly consistent with the ranges of estimates found in the economics literature.

If the Federal Reserve does not try to offset the effects of an increase in aggregate demand by raising short-term interest rates, the effect of that increase on output is both larger and less protracted. In such unusual circumstances, CBO uses demand multipliers that range from 0.5 to 2.5 over four quarters, and because there is no impact of changes in short-term interest rates, CBO projects no further effects on output in the short term. The low end of that range reflects the possibility that, as a result of fiscal stimulus or other increase in aggregate demand, other spending in the economy is reduced by as much as half of the direct effect—that is, private-sector spending is reduced by $0.50 for every $1.00 of the initial increase in demand. The high end of the range indicates that private activity is stimulated by fiscal stimulus or other increase in aggregate demand, generating an additional $1.50 of other spending per $1.00 of the initial increase in demand.

The upper portions of those ranges of demand multipliers are based mainly on macroeconometric models. The lower ends of those ranges are based mainly on time series models. Both ends of the ranges were adjusted outward slightly to reflect the uncertainty that underlies the estimates from different models.

IV. Demand Multipliers from Macroeconometric Forecasting Models

CBO draws heavily on macroeconometric forecasting models when analyzing the short-term effects on output of changes in fiscal policies. In particular, CBO draws on versions of the commercial forecasting models of two economic consulting firms—Macroeconomic Advisers and

IHS Global Insight—and on the FRB-US model used at the Federal Reserve Board. Those models incorporate the assumption that the economy has an underlying potential output determined by the size of the labor supply, the capital stock, and technology. They also reflect the assumption that actual output can change relative to potential output because of shifts in aggregate demand for goods and services from households, businesses, and the government. Those macroeconometric forecasting models produced a range of demand multipliers from 0.75 to 2.0 under normal economic conditions and from 1.25 to 2.25 when the Federal Reserve does not change monetary policy to try to offset the effects of fiscal policy.

The strengths of macroeconometric forecasting models include that their details are based largely on historical relationships among aggregate economic variables and that they are guided by economic theory. The latter feature helps the economists who construct such models to distinguish between statistical correlation and economic causation; it also allows the models to be adapted to reflect economic conditions that are not typical of past history (such as an inability of the Federal Reserve to adjust interest rates in response to changes in fiscal policies). However, the predictions of such models rely on the assumption that individuals will, on average, continue to react to changes in fiscal policies in the same way that they reacted in the past. Consequently, the models might not provide accurate predictions in the face of new policies.

Modeling Approaches and Estimates of Demand Multipliers

Macroeconomic forecasting models are used widely, and they underlie most of the forecasts offered to the clients of economic consulting firms. In addition, the models that CBO uses generally produce economic forecasts that are roughly in line with the consensus of private-sector forecasters, as compiled in the *Blue Chip Economic Indicators*. The details of interactions among economic variables in the models are based largely on historical relationships, informed by theories of how those variables are determined (for example, the theory that total consumer spending depends mostly on disposable income, wealth, and interest rates). Those features of macroeconometric forecasting models represent a contrast with time series models, which rely mostly on historical relationships, and with dynamic general-equilibrium models, which rely mostly on theory. Macroeconometric forecasting models also differ from other models by using less aggregated data than time series models and dynamic general-equilibrium models.[8] Because macroeconometric forecasting models emphasize the influence of aggregate demand on output in the short term, they tend to predict greater economic effects from policies that bolster demand than time series models and dynamic general-equilibrium models do.

The upper portions of CBO's ranges of demand multipliers are informed by macroeconometric models. For example, when interest rates are at their zero lower bound, estimates of demand multipliers generated using those models are roughly consistent with the upper end of the range CBO uses for such cases.[9] In contrast, under normal economic conditions, an increase in aggregate demand would generally lead to a rise in interest rates, which would crowd out some amount of spending.[10] CBO expects that such crowding out would offset roughly two-thirds of the cumulative impact of an increase in aggregate demand on GDP; the low and high ends of CBO's range of demand multipliers during normal economic conditions (measured over eight quarters to allow for

---

[8] See Fair (2010) for further discussion.

[9] For example, Fair (2010) uses a multicountry macroeconometric model to estimate the macroeconomic effects of ARRA and estimates a multiplier of 2.1. In addition, Blinder and Zandi (2010), using a model of the U.S. economy developed by Moody's Analytics, a consulting firm, and Macroeconomic Advisers (2009), using that firm's own model, estimate demand multipliers that range from about 1.5 to 2.0.

[10] Spending could also be crowded out through other channels besides an increase in interest rates. For example, activities spurred by stimulative fiscal policies could reduce production elsewhere in the economy if they used scarce materials or workers with specific skills and thereby created bottlenecks that hindered other production. As with crowding out caused by rising short-term interest rates, crowding out caused by production bottlenecks has probably been much smaller during the recent economic downturn (because of high unemployment and a large amount of unused capital) than it might be during other periods. Another channel for crowding out is that some people will respond to a fiscal stimulus by cutting back their spending in anticipation of higher taxes in the future. This channel is captured at least to some extent in macroeconometric forecasting models through the fact that households are predicted to save part of any change in their after-tax income.

the effects of rising interest rates) are roughly one-third of the low and high ends of CBO's range during periods when interest rates rise in response to an increase in aggregate demand.

Limitations

Macroeconometric forecasting models are based on economic principles, and the reliability of the models' predictions depends heavily on the validity of the specific economic assumptions used. Because the models are based largely on observed historical relationships among aggregate economic variables, their predictions rely on the assumption that individuals will, on average, continue to react to changes in fiscal policies in the same way that they reacted in the past. Consequently, the predictions might be unreliable when policies differ substantially from those used in the past.[11]

V. Demand Multipliers from Time Series Models

Economists use time series models to examine how economic variables such as output and consumption have behaved in the past relative to government spending and revenues. Those models can be used to analyze the effects of fiscal policies that have already been implemented and to project how similar policies might affect the economy in the future. CBO's ranges of demand multipliers are informed by the results of time series models. Such models have produced estimates of demand multipliers that generally range from 0.3 to 1.2, although recent analyses that account for differences in economic conditions have produced estimated demand multipliers of zero during economic expansions and from 3.0 to 3.5 during recessions.[12]

---

[11] See Parker (2011) and Auerbach and coauthors (2010) for a discussion of the limitations that arise from the use of historical data to estimate how output responds to new and untested fiscal policies.

[12] See Ramey (2011a) and Hall (2009) for summaries and discussions of research using time series models to estimate demand multipliers. For the first range cited in the text, the low-end estimate of 0.3 is from Mountford and Uhlig (2009), and the high-end estimate of 1.2 is from Monacelli and coauthors (2010). One analysis that accounts for economic conditions is Auerbach

It is unclear how estimates from time series models should be applied during times when the Federal Reserve is constrained by the zero lower bound, as it has been for the past few years. Many of the estimated multipliers are based on historical periods that include times when the Federal Reserve did not attempt to offset the effects of changes in fiscal policies by the federal government. However, the models are typically not explicit about how Federal Reserve actions affect demand multipliers during other times.

A strength of time series models is that they do not depend heavily on assumptions from potentially incorrect economic theories. However, the lack of a clear economic foundation also limits the usefulness of time series models for predicting the effects of fiscal policies when economic conditions differ from those typically observed in the past.

Modeling Approaches and Estimates of Demand Multipliers

In their most basic form, time series models summarize correlations between economic variables—such as government spending and GDP—over time.[13] However, they typically do not identify the direction of causation between policies and the economy. Examining correlations without imposing economic theories is a strength of time series models when there is reason to believe that the existing theories may be inaccurate or that their assumptions are particularly unrealistic. However, a lack of theory can make it difficult to assess what would happen under different economic conditions and to assess the direction of causation between economic variables. For example, poor economic conditions can lead the government to enact a policy such as ARRA in an effort to

---

and Gorodnichenko (2012), who estimate demand multipliers for changes in defense spending of zero during expansions and 3.0 during recessions. Those authors also estimate output multipliers (which are the product of the direct effects and the demand multiplier) for nondefense spending, consumption spending, and investment spending that range from zero to 1.0 during economic expansions and from zero to 2.0 during recessions. In a separate analysis, Auerbach and Gorodnichenko (2011) use data for a large number of countries in the Organisation for Economic Co-operation and Development (OECD), which includes the United States, to estimate a demand multiplier of 3.5.

[13] An often used form of such time series models is a vector autoregression (VAR) model.

stimulate economic activity; it would then be incorrect to conclude from a statistical correlation that the policy caused the weak economic performance.[14] Likewise, if states and localities reduced purchases and laid employees off when their budgets deteriorated in a recession, it would not be accurate to blame the recession on the cuts in government spending. Thus, when causation runs in both directions in this way, the historical correlation between variables is not always the best guide for predicting the effects of a new policy proposal.

Two approaches are often used to identify economic causation as distinct from pure statistical correlation. One approach relies entirely on statistical assumptions about the interaction of the economic variables of interest.[15] That approach is easy to implement (because it does not require the specification of many behavioral relationships or extensive data gathering) and is useful when the statistical assumptions are correct. However, if the statistical assumptions are incorrect, then the approach may lead to less reliable estimates of demand multipliers than the most basic form of time series models.

An alternative approach supplements the time series analysis of aggregate data with a review of historical evidence of other sorts—such as narrative evidence from the *Congressional Record*. That narrative approach has been used most often to estimate the economic impact of unanticipated military buildups prior to armed conflicts—events that are arguably unrelated to macroeconomic conditions and therefore allow the narrative approach to avoid the problem of causation running in

---

[14] See Leeper (2010) for a discussion of the complexities involved in using time series models to estimate the economic effects of fiscal policy.

[15] This approach is called structural vector autoregression (SVAR). For a discussion of the approach, see Blanchard and Perotti (2002). They argue that the direction of causation between government policies and GDP can be revealed by making assumptions about how fiscal policy can respond to changes in GDP, and they find an output multiplier of 0.6 after an unanticipated increase in government spending. Using this approach, Monacelli and coauthors (2010) estimate a multiplier of 1.2 and Mountford and Uhlig (2009) estimate a multiplier of 0.3.

both directions.[16] Recent studies examining the impact of such buildups typically estimate multipliers between 0.4 and 0.9.[17]

A drawback of estimating demand multipliers using time series models is that there are relatively few episodes of large increases in government spending that are not related to economic conditions.[18] Demand multipliers estimated using military buildups depend almost entirely on two war episodes—World War II and the Korean War. During both of those eras, resources in the U.S. economy were more fully employed than they have been in the past few years. In addition, during World War II, rationing and price controls were in effect, civilian plants were dedicated to military purposes, and taxes were increased dramatically—all of which might have reduced the positive indirect effects of government spending on private consumption and investment. Moreover, the Korean War buildup was correlated with a much longer-term buildup in military spending in support of the Cold War.[19]

---

[16] Ramey (2011b) highlights the importance of measuring anticipation effects, which are the responses by households to expected spending or tax changes. If anticipation effects are not measured correctly, the estimated demand multipliers may not reflect the actual responses of the economy to fiscal policy shocks. Leeper and coauthors (2012) provide a discussion of how to measure news about fiscal policy over time.

[17] See Ramey (2012), Barro and Redlick (2011), Ramey (2011a), Ramey (2011b), Hall (2009), and Ramey and Shapiro (1998). See also Fisher and Peters (2010), which estimates a cumulative multiplier of 1.5 over five years using stock returns related to defense companies.

[18] A related literature uses the narrative approach to estimate the effects of tax changes on economic activity (expressed as a tax multiplier). For example, Romer and Romer (2010) estimate a tax multiplier of roughly 1 after four quarters; Favero and Giavazzi (2012) estimate a tax multiplier of roughly 0.5; Mertens and Ravan (2012) estimate tax multipliers of roughly 1.0 for unanticipated tax cuts and 0.1 for anticipated tax cuts; and Perotti (2012) finds a tax multiplier of 1.2 (after six quarters). Because tax multipliers are the product of the direct effects of tax changes on demand and the demand multiplier, tax multipliers have to be adjusted before comparing them to the demand multipliers estimated in other studies. Based on its review of the evidence, CBO expects that the direct effects of temporary tax cuts range from 0.2 to 0.6 and the direct effects of permanent tax cuts range from 0.5 to 0.9. Based on those values, estimates of tax multipliers would have to be multiplied by a factor ranging from 1.1 to 5.0 to be comparable to estimates of demand multipliers. A recent analysis by Chahrour and coauthors (2012) of the SVAR and narrative approaches concludes that it is unclear whether those two approaches estimate the true economic effects of tax changes.

[19] For further discussion of the limitations of time series models that estimate demand multipliers by examining military buildups, see Parker (2011), Ramey (2011a), Auerbach and coauthors (2010), and Hall (2009). Ramey (2011a) argues that interest rates in the United States were held virtually constant during the 1939–1947 period—which could produce multipliers similar to those that would arise with interest rates at the zero lower bound—and that multipliers were not higher during that period than during other periods. She concludes that demand multipliers may not be higher during times of constant interest rates than during normal economic conditions.

As a way to address the data limitation associated with research focused at the national level, another line of research uses time series models to study the economic effects of changes in fiscal policies on counties, states, and regions in the United States.[20] That research generally estimates demand multipliers—often called subnational or local multipliers to reflect that they are not generated by countrywide data—that are considerably larger than studies for the nation as a whole, typically in the range from 1.5 to 3.4.[21] A subset of such research uses data available at the state level to study the economic effects of ARRA (or some of its provisions).[22] Analyzing variations in the allocation of ARRA funds across states, such research estimates demand multipliers that range from zero to 3.4, with the majority of estimates close to 2.0.[23]

However, demand multipliers estimated using data from counties, states, and regions are of limited applicability when the ultimate aim is to calculate the economic effects of changes in fiscal policies for the entire U.S. economy. One reason is that the estimation of such local multipliers cannot account for spillovers from recipient states to other states (such as shifts in resources from other

---

[20] The literature using state and local data in such time series models is diverse. For example, Clemens and Miran (2012) use differences in state budget practices, including variations in their balanced-budget requirements; Nakamura and Steinsson (2011) study regional variations in military spending by the federal government; Reingewertz (2011) uses variations in the party affiliation of states' Congressional delegations; Shoag (2011) considers state-level variations in returns of state pension funds; and Serrato and Wingender (2011) use county-level variations in federal spending allocated on the basis of population estimates.

[21] Clemens and Miran (2012) and Conley and Dupor (2011) are exceptions. Clemens and Miran estimate multipliers that are generally less than 1. As they argue, their methodology captures the tendency for deficits to crowd out private spending, a feature ignored by most research estimating subnational multipliers. Conley and Dupor find that ARRA decreased private employment enough to fully offset the increases in state and local government employment it created, implying a subnational multiplier of zero; however, their estimates are measured with so much imprecision that their results are not very helpful in uncovering the economic effects of ARRA.

[22] See Chodorow-Reich and coauthors (forthcoming), Wilson (forthcoming), Conley and Dupor (2011), and Feyrer and Sacerdote (2011).

[23] State and local data have also been used to investigate the direct effects of ARRA. For example, Taylor (2011) and Cogan and Taylor (2010) find that most of the ARRA grants to states and localities were used to decrease net borrowing rather than to increase purchases. As a result, they conclude that the increase in government purchases due to ARRA grants given to states was close to zero. Chodorow-Reich and coauthors (forthcoming) offer a different perspective, concluding that at least some of the ARRA funds they examined (Medicaid matching funds) were used to avoid deeper cuts in spending and employment. (From January 2009 through December 2011, the workforce of state and local governments contracted by about 17,000 employees per month, on average, or about 621,000 employees for that period. In comparison, over the 10-year period prior to 2009, state and local governments added roughly 21,000 employees per month to their payrolls.) An unresolved question in the literature on ARRA's direct effects on state and local spending is the extent to which states and localities could have borrowed to finance certain expenditures. For a discussion of the fiscal issues faced by local governments after the recent recession, see Congressional Budget Office (2010b).

states or increases in demand for output from other states). Another reason is that local multipliers do not fully account for nationwide crowding out of investment, because such crowding out would dampen output regardless of whether a state benefited directly from changes in federal fiscal policies.[24] Translating local multipliers into multipliers for the country as a whole requires making assumptions about, among other things, the responsiveness of interest rates to fiscal policy. The demand multipliers for the country obtained in this way may reflect modeling assumptions more than the actual effects of fiscal policy on the aggregate economy.[25]

A recent strand of research uses time series models to consider how the demand multiplier varies over the business cycle. Using time series models that differentiate between recessions and expansions, researchers have estimated that the demand multiplier during recessions ranges from 3.0 to 3.5 but the demand multiplier during expansions is close to zero.[26]

Limitations

All varieties of time series models share at least one common limitation: They do not include explicit assumptions about how individuals and businesses make economic decisions. Such models, although grounded in historical data, might not provide accurate predictions in the face of new policies or new circumstances. Another limitation is that most time series models do not allow multipliers to vary over the business cycle, although there are reasons to believe that changes in

---

[24] For a further discussion of this matter, see Clemens and Miran (2012).

[25] See Nakamura and Steinsson (2011).

[26] See Auerbach and Gorodnichenko (2012) and Auerbach and Gorodnichenko (2011). The multipliers cited in the text are cumulative multipliers over a four-quarter period, consistent with CBO's definition of the demand multiplier. Auerbach and Gorodnichenko (2012) also report peak multipliers that, depending on assumptions, range from 0.5 to 1.1 during economic expansions and from 3.1 to 7.1 during recessions. Those findings reinforce Auerbach and Gorodnichenko (2011), who use national data for a number of countries in the OECD. They report an estimate of the demand multiplier for the U.S. economy during recessions of 3.5. For an analysis of multipliers over the business cycle using a model of the labor market, see Michaillat (2012). For further discussion of the size of demand multipliers over the business cycle, see International Monetary Fund (2012).

fiscal policies will have different effects during economic booms than during periods of economic weakness.[27]

VI. Demand Multipliers from Dynamic General-Equilibrium Models

Dynamic general-equilibrium models (DGE models) are often used to study business cycles as well as the economic effects of changes in fiscal policies. While CBO does not rely heavily on the estimates of demand multipliers from DGE models, the agency uses those models to help understand the economic mechanisms that underlie estimates in the empirical literature and to gauge how changes in business and consumer behavior may affect multipliers. In the simplified forms of such models, increases in government spending or decreases in taxes tend to crowd out a significant amount of other economic activity, which means that the demand multipliers implied by those models tend to be less than 1. However, in more-complex forms of such models that incorporate more realistic features, the demand multipliers can be considerably larger than 1. DGE models have produced a range of demand multipliers from 0.5 to 1.5 under normal economic conditions and from 0.7 to 2.5 when the Federal Reserve does not change monetary policy to try to offset the effects of fiscal policy.

A strength of DGE models is that they are rooted firmly in economic theory and incorporate explicit assumptions about how individuals and businesses make economic decisions. A limitation of DGE models is that the results of such models are affected in significant ways by the specific assumptions used in their construction.[28]

---

[27] See Parker (2011) and Auerbach and coauthors (2010) for a more detailed discussion of the limitations of time series models.

[28] DGE models are generally calibrated so that macroeconomic variables, such as the total amount of labor supplied and the size of the capital stock, match the amounts in the U.S. economy, or they are estimated using aggregate data to determine some key parameters. See Fernández-Villaverde and Rubio-Ramírez (2006) for a detailed discussion of how DGE models are estimated.

Modeling Approaches and Estimates of Demand Multipliers

In DGE models, people are assumed to make decisions about how much to work, buy, and save on the basis of current and expected future values of wage rates, interest rates, taxes, and government purchases, among other things. As a result of those and other assumptions about individuals' and businesses' behavior, such models offer a clear perspective on the causal relationships among economic variables.

That grounding in economic theory allows DGE models to avoid the difficulties of interpretation that arise with purely statistical approaches to analyzing data. In addition, the explicit assumptions about economic decision-making in such models can be particularly useful when analyzing the effects of changes in fiscal policies that have not been observed previously. However, different assumptions about that decision-making or about other aspects of the workings of the economy can produce a wide range of predicted effects of changes in fiscal policies.

For example, DGE models usually do not allow for underutilized resources in an economy, such as involuntary unemployment or unused capital. In addition, people are generally assumed to have full access to credit markets so that they can borrow to maintain their consumption in the face of a temporary loss of income, and the Federal Reserve is generally assumed to respond to changes in fiscal policies (thereby excluding the situation in the past several years where actions by the Federal Reserve have been constrained by the zero lower bound on nominal interest rates). Moreover, DGE models are typically built on the assumptions that people have full information about the current economy and future economic developments and that they logically base their current decisions on a full lifetime plan. In extreme form, those assumptions imply that people

---

See Coenen and coauthors (2012) for a comparison of significant model features and parameters of several DGE models used by policymaking institutions in Canada, Europe, and the United States.

perfectly anticipate that any increase in government spending or decrease in taxes will eventually lead to lower spending or higher taxes and that they raise their current saving enough to offset that expected future burden. Therefore, in such models, cash transfer payments and many sorts of reductions in taxes usually have little or no effect on current spending.

In an effort to align DGE models more closely with important aspects of the economy, recent research has introduced significant new features into such models. One feature is the addition of so-called hand-to-mouth consumers (or liquidity-constrained consumers or rule-of-thumb consumers). Research on consumer behavior has found that the spending of some households tends to vary one-for-one with income, perhaps in part because those households have only small savings and face borrowing constraints and therefore cannot maintain their desired level of consumption when their incomes fall, and in part because those households follow simple behavior rules rather than trying to continuously determine their optimal spending and saving. Recent estimates of demand multipliers generated using DGE models with hand-to-mouth consumers range from 0.5 to 1.5 and are as much as 50 percent larger than multiplier estimates generated using standard DGE models.[29]

Another important new feature that has been introduced into some DGE models is the possibility of monetary policy that keeps short-term interest rates close to the zero lower bound.[30] Such models have generated demand multipliers that range from 0.7 to 2.5.[31] Those models also show that the timing of increases in government spending or reductions in taxes is important. Several

---

[29] See Coenen and coauthors (2012), Christiano and coauthors (2011), Davig and Leeper (2011), Eggertsson (20011), Woodford (2011), Forni and coauthors (2009), Hall (2009), Leeper and coauthors (2009), Ratto and coauthors (2009), and Galí and coauthors (2007).

[30] Additional research has relaxed other standard assumptions of DGE models. For example, Fernández-Villaverde (2010) develops a model that incorporates financial frictions, and Leeper and coauthors (2009) study the economic effects of productive government investment.

[31] See Coenen and coauthors (2012), Christiano and coauthors (2011), Davig and Leeper (2011), Eggertsson (2011), Woodford (2011), Cogan and coauthors (2010), and Hall (2009).

recent studies find that if such policy changes occur entirely in periods when the short-term interest rate is at the zero lower bound, the size of the demand multiplier is roughly two to three times larger than when only half of the changes occur under those conditions.[32]

Limitations

The predictions of DGE models for the effects of changes in fiscal policies depend on the assumptions about economic behavior that are built into the models. Common assumptions in DGE models about consumers' spending and saving decisions, about monetary policy, and about the availability of underutilized resources may not be realistic, and they affect predicted demand multipliers in significant ways. Furthermore, to facilitate the use of DGE models, analysts often use highly aggregated data, which may lead to misleading conclusions.[33]

---

[32] See, for example, Coenen and coauthors (2012) and Christiano and coauthors (2011). Cogan and coauthors (2010) assume that only a small fraction of an increase in government spending would occur when the short-term interest rate is at the zero lower bound and that the rest would occur after the short-term interest rate begins to rise; they estimate demand multipliers that are considerably smaller than those estimated by others who consider interest rates that remain near zero for an extended period.

[33] For example, see Parker (2011) and Fair (2012), who criticize several modeling choices made in many DGE models. In addition, Leeper and coauthors (2011) observe that a tight range for estimates of the demand multiplier is imposed by the assumptions and choices made by researchers when using DGE models. See also Chari and coauthors (2009), who argue that DGE models rely on so many improvised modeling assumptions that their conclusions are unavoidably ambiguous for policy analysis.

VII. References

Alesina, Alberto and Silvia Ardagna. 1998. "Tales of Fiscal Adjustment." *Economic Policy*, 13 (27): 487–545.

Auerbach, Alan J., William G. Gale, and Benjamin H. Harris. 2010. "Activist Fiscal Policy." *Journal of Economic Perspectives*, 24 (4): 141–164.

Auerbach, Alan J. and Yuriy Gorodnichenko. 2011. "Fiscal Multipliers in Recession and Expansion." National Bureau of Economic Research Working Paper 17447.

Auerbach, Alan J. and Yuriy Gorodnichenko. 2012. "Measuring the Output Responses to Fiscal Policy." *American Economic Journal: Economic Policy*, 4 (2): 1–27.

Barro, Robert J. and Charles J. Redlick. 2011. "Macroeconomic Effects from Government Purchases and Taxes." *The Quarterly Journal of Economics*, 126 (1): 51–102.

Blanchard, Olivier and Roberto Perotti. 2002. "An Empirical Characterization of the Dynamic Effects of Changes in Government Spending and Taxes on Output." *The Quarterly Journal of Economics*, 117 (4): 1329–1368.

Blinder, Alan S., and Mark Zandi. 2010. "How the Great Recession Was Brought to an End." Unpublished.

Bloom, Nicholas. 2009. "The Impact of Uncertainty Shocks." *Econometrica*, 77 (3): 623–685.

Chahrour, Ryan, Stephanie Schmitt-Grohé, and Martín Uribe. 2012. "A Model-Based Evaluation of the Debate on the Size of the Tax Multiplier." *American Economic Journal: Economic Policy*, 4 (2): 28–45.

Chari, V. V., Patrick J. Kehoe, and Ellen R. McGrattan. 2009. "New Keynesian Models: Not Yet Useful for Policy Analysis." *American Economic Journal: Macroeconomics*, 1 (1): 242–266.

Chodorow-Reich, Gabriel, Laura Feiveson, Zachary Liscow, and William Gui Woolston. Forthcoming. "Does State Fiscal Relief During Recessions Increase Employment? Evidence from the American Recovery and Reinvestment Act." *American Economic Journal: Economic Policy*.

Christiano, Lawrence, Martin Eichenbaum, and Sergio Rebelo. 2011. "When is the Government Spending Multiplier Large?" *Journal of Political Economy*, 119 (1): 78–121.

Clemens, Jeffrey Paul and Stephen I. Miran. 2012. "Fiscal Policy Multipliers on Sub-National Government Spending." *American Economic Journal: Economic Policy*, 4 (2): 46-68.

Coenen, Günter, Christopher Erceg, Charles Freedman, Davide Furceri, Michael Kumhof, René Lalonde, Douglas Laxton, Jesper Lind, Annabelle Mourougane, Dirk Muir, Susanna Mursula, Carlos de Resende, John Roberts, Werner Roeger, Stephen Snudden, Mathias Trabandt, and Jan in't Veld. 2012. "Effects of Fiscal Stimulus in Structural Models." *American Economic Journal: Macroeconomics*, 4 (1): 22–68.

Cogan, John F., Tobias Cwik, John B. Taylor, and Volker Wieland. 2010. "New Keynesian Versus Old Keynesian Government Spending Multipliers." *Journal of Economic Dynamics and Control*, 34 (3): 281–295.

Cogan, John F. and John B. Taylor. 2010. "What the Government Purchases Multiplier Actually Multiplied in the 2009 Stimulus Package." National Bureau of Economic Research Working Paper 16505.

Congressional Budget Office. 2010a. "The Economic Outlook and Fiscal Policy Choices."

Congressional Budget Office. 2010b. "Fiscal Stress Faced by Local Governments."

Congressional Budget Office. 2011a. "Policies for Increasing Economic Growth and Employment in 2012 and 2013."

Congressional Budget Office. 2011b. "The Macroeconomic and Budgetary Effects of an Illustrative Policy for Reducing the Federal Budget Deficit."

Congressional Budget Office. 2012a. "Budget and Economic Outlook: Fiscal Years 2012 to 2022."

Congressional Budget Office. 2012b. "Estimated Impact of the American Recovery and Reinvestment Act on Employment and Economic Output From October 2011 Through December 2011."

Congressional Budget Office. 2012c. "The Economic Impact of the President's 2013 Budget."

Congressional Budget Office. 2012d. "The Long-Term Budgetary Impact of Paths for Federal Revenues and Spending Specified by Chairman Ryan."

Conley, Timothy and Bill Dupor. 2011. "The American Recovery and Reinvestment Act: Public Sector Jobs Saved, Private Sector Jobs Forestalled." Unpublished.

Davig, Troy and Eric M. Leeper. 2011. "Monetary-Fiscal Policy Interactions and Fiscal Stimulus." *European Economic Review*, 55 (2): 211–227.

Eggertsson, Gauti B. 2011. "What Fiscal Policy Is Effective at Zero Interest Rates?" *NBER Macroeconomics Annual*, 25 (1): 59–112.

Fair, Ray C. 2010. "Estimated Macroeconomic Effects of the U.S. Stimulus Bill." *Contemporary Economic Policy*, 28 (4): 439–452.

Fair, Ray C. 2012. "Has macro progressed?" *Journal of Macroeconomics*, 34 (1): 2–10.

Favero, Carlo and Francesco Giavazzi. 2012. "Measuring Tax Multipliers: The Narrative Method in Fiscal VARs." *American Economic Journal: Economic Policy*, 4 (2): 69–94.

Fernández-Villaverde, Jesús. 2010. "Fiscal Policy in a Model with Financial Frictions." *American Economic Review: Papers & Proceedings*, 100 (2): 35–40.

Fernández-Villaverde, Jesús and Juan F. Rubio-Ramírez. 2006. "Our Research Agenda: Estimating DSGE Models." Unpublished.

Feyrer, James and Bruce Sacerdote. 2011. "Did the Stimulus Stimulate? Real Time Estimates of the Effects of the American Recovery and Readjustment Act." National Bureau of Economic Research Working Paper 16759.

Fisher, Jonas D. M. and Ryan Peters. 2010. "Using Stock Returns to Identify Government Spending Shocks." *Economic Journal*, 120 (544): 414–436.

Forni, Lorenzo, Libero Monteforte, and Luca Sessa. 2009. "The General Equilibrium Effects of Fiscal Policy: Estimates for the Euro Area." *Journal of Public Economics*, 93 (3-4): 559–585.

Galí, Jordi, J. David López-Salido, and Javier Vallés. 2007. "Understanding the Effects of Government Spending on Consumption." *Journal of the European Economic Association*, 5 (1): 227–270.

Hall, Robert E. 2009. "By How Much Does GDP Rise If the Government Buys More Output?" *Brookings Papers on Economic Activity: Fall 2009*, (2): 183–249.

International Monetary Fund. 2010. *World Economic Outlook: Recovery, Risk, and Rebalancing*, Washington, D.C. Chapter 3.

International Monetary Fund. 2012. *Fiscal Monitor: Balancing Fiscal Policy Risk*, Washington, D.C. Appendix 1.

Leeper, Eric M. 2010. "Monetary Science, Fiscal Alchemy." in *Macroeconomic Challenges: The Decade Ahead*, Federal Reserve Bank of Kansas City Jackson Hole Symposium.

Leeper, Eric M., Alexander W. Richter, and Todd B. Walker. 2012. "Quantitative Effects of Fiscal Foresight." *American Economic Journal: Economic Policy*, 4 (2): 115–144.

Leeper, Eric M., Nora Traum, and Todd B. Walker. 2011. "Clearing Up the Fiscal Multiplier Morass." National Bureau of Economic Research Working Paper 17444.

Leeper, Eric M., Todd B. Walker, and Shu-Chun Susan Yang. 2009. "Government Investment and Fiscal Stimulus in the Short and Long Runs." National Bureau of Economic Research Working Paper 15153.

Macroeconomics Advisers. 2009. "Fiscal Stimulus to the Rescue?" *Macroeconomic Advisers' Macro Focus*, 4 (1): 1–10.

Mertens, Karel and Morten O. Ravn. 2012. "Empirical Evidence on the Aggregate Effects of Anticipated and Unanticipated US Tax Policy Shocks." *American Economic Journal: Economic Policy*, 4 (2): 145–181.

Michaillat, Pascal. 2012. "Fiscal Multipliers over the Business Cycle." Centre for Economic Performance Discussion Paper 1115.

Monacelli, Tommaso, Roberto Perotti, and Antonella Trigari. 2010. "Unemployment Fiscal Multipliers." *Journal of Monetary Economics*, 57 (5): 531–553.

Mountford, Andrew and Harald Uhlig. 2009. "What are the Effects of Fiscal Policy Shocks?" *Journal of Applied Econometrics*, 24 (6): 960–992.

Nakamura, Emi and Jón Steinsson. 2011. "Fiscal Stimulus in a Monetary Union: Evidence from U.S. Regions." National Bureau of Economic Research Working Paper 17391.

Parker, Jonathan A. 2011. "On Measuring the Effects of Fiscal Policy in Recessions." *Journal of Economic Literature*, 49 (3): 703–718.

Perotti, Roberto. 2012. "The Effects of Tax Shocks on Output: Not So Large, but Not Small Either." *American Economic Journal: Economic Policy*, 4 (2): 214–237.

Ramey, Valerie A. 2011a. "Can Government Purchases Stimulate the Economy?" *Journal of Economic Literature*, 49 (3): 673–685.

Ramey, Valerie A. 2011b. "Identifying Government Spending Shocks: It's All in the Timing." *The Quarterly Journal of Economics*, 126 (1): 1–50.

Ramey, Valerie A. 2012. "Government Spending and Private Activity." National Bureau of Economic Research Working Paper 17787.

Ramey, Valerie A. and Matthew D. Shapiro. 1998. "Costly Capital Reallocation and the Effects of Government Spending." *Carnegie-Rochester Conference Series on Public Policy*, 48 (1): 145–194.

Ratto, Marco, Werner Roeger, and Jan in't Veld. 2009. "QUEST III: An Estimated Open-Economy DSGE Model of the Euro Area with Fiscal and Monetary Policy." *Economic Modelling*, 26 (1): 222–233.

Reingewertz, Yaniv. 2011. "Identifying the Effect of Government Spending: Evidence from Political Variations in Federal Grants." Unpublished.

Romer, Christina D. and David H. Romer. 2010. "The Macroeconomic Effects of Tax Changes: Estimates Based on a New Measure of Fiscal Shocks." *American Economic Review*, 100 (3): 763–801.

Serrato, Juan Carlos Suárez and Philippe Wingender. 2011. "Estimating Local Fiscal Multipliers." Unpublished.

Shoag, Daniel. 2010. "The Impact of Government Spending Shocks: Evidence on the Multiplier from State Pension Plan Returns." Unpublished.

Taylor, John B. 2011. "An Empirical Analysis of the Revival of Fiscal Activism in the 2000s." *Journal of Economic Literature*, 49 (3): 686–702.

Wilson, Daniel J. Forthcoming. "Fiscal Spending Jobs Multipliers: Evidence from the 2009 American Recovery and Reinvestment Act." *American Economic Journal: Economic Policy*.

Woodford, Michael. 2011. "Simple Analytics of the Government Expenditure Multiplier." *American Economic Journal: Macroeconomics*, 3 (1): 1–35.

www.ingramcontent.com/pod-product-compliance
Lightning Source LLC
Chambersburg PA
CBHW081823170526
45167CB00008B/3521